ROCHESTER HILLS
PUBLIC LIBRARY
500 Olde Towne Road
Rochester, MI 48307
(248) 656-2900

PERSPECTIVES ON THE DUST BOWL

by Amy C. Rea

3 3158 00996 5291

www.12StoryLibrary.com

Copyright © 2018 by 12-Story Library, Mankato, MN 56003. All rights reserved. No part of this book may be reproduced or utilized in any form or by any means without written permission from the publisher.

12-Story Library is an imprint of Bookstaves and Press Room Editions

Produced for 12-Story Library by Red Line Editorial

Photographs ©: AP Images, cover, 1, 4, 6, 7, 16, 20, 23, 29; Arthur Rothstein/Farm Security Administration/Office of War Information Black-and-White Negatives/Library of Congress, 5, 8, 14; Russell Lee/Farm Security Administration/Office of War Information Black-and-White Negatives/Library of Congress, 9; Everett Historical/Shutterstock Images, 10, 11; World History Archive/Newscom, 13, 27; Dorothea Lange/Farm Security Administration/Office of War Information Black-and-White Negatives/Library of Congress, 15, 17, 18, 19, 21, 25, 28; Harris & Ewing/Harris & Ewing Collection/Library of Congress, 24; Al Aumuller/New York World-Telegram and the Sun Newspaper Photograph Collection/Library of Congress, 26

Content Consultant: Pamela Riney-Kehrberg, Professor, Department of History, Iowa State University

Library of Congress Cataloging-in-Publication Data
Names: Rea, Amy C., author.
Title: Perspectives on the Dust Bowl / by Amy C. Rea.
Description: Mankato, MN : 12-Story Library, [2018] | Series: Perspectives on
  US history | Includes bibliographical references and index.
Identifiers: LCCN 2016047346 (print) | LCCN 2016059914 (ebook) | ISBN
  9781632353993 (hardcover : alkaline paper) | ISBN 9781632354716 (paperback
  : alkaline paper) | ISBN 9781621435235 (hosted e-book)
Subjects: LCSH: Dust Bowl Era, 1931-1939--Juvenile literature. | Dust
  storms--Great Plains--History--20th century--Juvenile literature. |
  Droughts--Great Plains--History--20th century--Juvenile literature. |
  Great Plains--History--20th century--Juvenile literature.
Classification: LCC F595 .R28 2018 (print) | LCC F595 (ebook) | DDC
  973.917--dc23
LC record available at https://lccn.loc.gov/2016047346

Printed in the United States of America
022017

ROCHESTER HILLS
PUBLIC LIBRARY
500 Olde Towne Road
Rochester, MI 48307
(248) 656-2900

Access free, up-to-date content on this topic plus a full digital version of this book. Scan the QR code on page 31 or use your school's login at 12StoryLibrary.com.

Table of Contents

Fact Sheet 4

Farmers Continue to Plant Crops 6

Families Struggle to Keep Homes Clean 8

Most Migrants Are Called Okies 10

Black People Move North or East Instead 12

Children Try to Stay Healthy 14

The Dust Bowl Affects More Than Farmers 16

California Residents Do Not Welcome Outsiders 18

California Government Tries to Stop Migrants 20

The US Government Finally Takes Action 22

The Media Begins to Pay Attention 24

Artists Want to Tell Dust Bowl Stories 26

California Farms Benefit from Law Exclusions 28

Glossary 30

For More Information 31

Index 32

About the Author 32

Fact Sheet

What was the Dust Bowl?

In the 1930s, droughts hit much of the US Great Plains. This area was known as the Dust Bowl. It covered more than 150,000 square miles (388,500 sq km) of the midwestern and southern United States. Soil was dried out as a result of overfarming and droughts. Strong winds whipped up the dry soil. This created dust storms called "black blizzards." The storms made daytime seem as dark as night.

How did the Dust Bowl happen?

World War I (1914–1918) created a big demand for wheat. Many people rushed to the Great Plains to farm. They tore up the prairie grasses to plant wheat and corn fields. The Great Depression hit at the end of the 1920s. Crop prices fell. Farmers tried planting more crops and clearing bigger fields. But prices continued to fall. Some people just walked away from their fields. A series of droughts made things worse. Without grass roots to hold it down, dry topsoil was blown away by the wind.

Who was affected by the Dust Bowl?

The droughts in the 1930s affected more than 75 percent of the United States. States impacted included Colorado, Kansas, Nebraska, New Mexico, Oklahoma, and Texas. Farmers lost millions of acres to the dust storms. Without a source of income, some farmers lost their homes.

The dust storms also made people sick. People would spit up clods of dirt. The disease was referred to as "dust pneumonia." By the time the Dust Bowl era ended in 1940, more than 2.5 million people had moved away from the Great Plains region.

1
Farmers Continue to Plant Crops

The drought and dust storms in the Dust Bowl region made farming impossible for many people. Some people had no choice but to leave their homes in search of a better life. But more often than not, farmers stayed. Some remained on their farms because they thought the dust storms would be over in a year or two. Others stayed because they could not afford to move.

Those who did stay kept trying to plant crops.

As the dust storms continued, the US government wanted to change the way farmers worked the land. Government agencies planted rows of trees to create windbreaks. They planted grasses on unused soil to hold the dirt in place. Farmers were supposed to use contour plowing or terraces on their land. That would help keep the dry soil from blowing away. The government

A dust storm advances on an Oklahoma ranch in 1935.

told farmers not to plant a portion of their farm each year. That would give the soil time to come back to life.

But the farmers were worried and skeptical. They had seen many people lose their homes. Farmers were not sure these farming methods would help. Government agencies sent scientists to work with the farmers. The scientists showed them how to use the different farming methods. Money from the government helped farmers who were in debt. By the end of the drought, most farmers wanted to continue using the methods.

This Oklahoma farmer could not grow any crops for more than six years.

35 million
Estimated acres (14.2 million ha) of Dust Bowl farmland damaged by 1934.

- Farmers stayed because they hoped the dust storms would end.
- The government used scientists and money to persuade farmers to try different methods.
- Farmers were wary at first, but most continued to use the new methods after the drought ended.

JACKRABBITS AND GRASSHOPPERS

The dust storms were bad enough. But in 1935, Dust Bowl residents also had to battle hordes of jackrabbits and grasshoppers. Swarms of grasshoppers destroyed any crops that survived the storms. Towns organized rabbit drives to kill the thousands of jackrabbits that also consumed crops.

2
Families Struggle to Keep Homes Clean

Life was hard for most families during the Great Depression. Those who lived in the Dust Bowl region had an even harder time. Family homes were covered in dirt after every dust storm. But the dust did not stay outside. Homes in the 1930s were not built tightly enough to keep the dust from getting in. This cleaning challenge fell mostly to women, who were responsible for a majority of the housework during this time.

Women spent a lot of time in the home trying to keep things as clean as

Even tiny cracks, such as the spaces between bricks, let dust into homes.

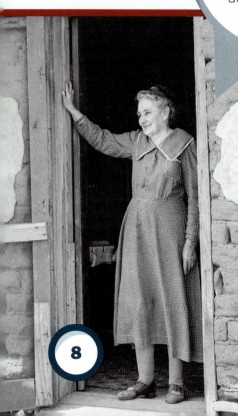

38
Number of dust storms in 1933.

- Women struggled to keep their homes clean as dust piled up inside.
- Women tried different cooking and baking methods, but dust still got into food.
- To help keep children healthy, women made them dust masks.

8

BLACK SUNDAY

There were many terrible dust storms, but the worst of all was on Sunday, April 14, 1935. It came to be known as "Black Sunday." The day started out with good weather. But then the temperature dropped by as much as 50 degrees Fahrenheit (10°C). People who were outside noticed that birds were gathering in their yards, making a lot of noise. Then the storm came. This storm alone carried away more than 300,000 tons (270,000 metric tons) of topsoil.

possible. They often had to remove buckets of dirt after each storm. Women would hang wet sheets over windows to try to keep the dust out. But little worked.

It was also hard for women to cook meals for their families. They tried baking food in the oven instead of cooking on the stove. Some kneaded bread dough inside a dresser drawer instead of on the counter. But no matter what, dust always seemed to get into the food.

The dust storms caused many illnesses. It was dangerous to constantly breathe in so much dust. Women tried to keep their children healthy. Some made dust masks for their children to wear to school. They hoped this would help prevent illness.

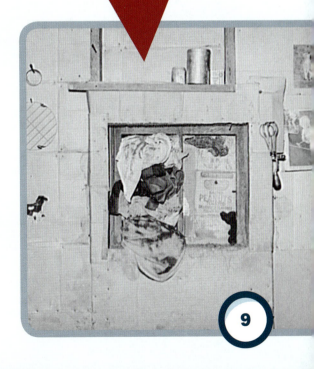

People stuffed cloth and newspapers into windows to try to keep the dust out.

3

Most Migrants Are Called Okies

Farmers in eastern Oklahoma fared somewhat better than people living in the Dust Bowl region. They did not face as many dust storms. But they were still affected by droughts. Crops did not grow as well. Farmers were still struggling because of the Great Depression.

By the mid-1930s, the US government began paying landowners not to grow crops. They hoped to reduce the supply so that farmers could charge better prices. But the majority of the farmers in Oklahoma did not own the land they worked. They rented it. Landowners who agreed not to grow crops kicked these renters off their properties.

Many people began to move west in 1935. Most looked for whatever jobs they could find. Somewhere between 300,000 and 400,000 people went to California to work in the fields. People from every part of the Dust Bowl region, not just Oklahoma, went to California. Despite this, most migrants were called Okies. It was not a friendly nickname. Okies were usually not welcome in California. Money was scarce there, too, because of the Great Depression. Californians thought that the Okies were

These migrants found work harvesting carrots in California.

10

Okies sometimes had to migrate by walking, carrying the few things they owned.

coming to take away their jobs and food. Some Californians put up signs reading, "Okie, go back. We don't want you."

The Okies often lived in camps on the side of the road or in fields. They looked for work in agriculture. Sometimes they would travel nearly 1,000 miles (1,600 km) in a single season, looking for work. They faced stiff job competition and low pay.

2.5 million
Number of people who had moved away from the Dust Bowl region by 1940.

- Many people who did not own land moved west during the Dust Bowl era.
- Many migrants moved to California.
- Migrants came from all over the Dust Bowl but were usually called Okies.
- Okies were not always welcome in California and had to compete with others for low-paying jobs.

THINK ABOUT IT
Why do you think so many people went to California? Why did that seem like a better choice than moving north or east?

4

Black People Move North or East Instead

Before the dust storms, black people living in the Dust Bowl region already experienced discrimination. The Great Depression also affected black people differently. They faced higher unemployment rates. By 1932, approximately half of all black people in the United States were unemployed.

Many white people felt that white people should be offered jobs before any black person. Black people also received less government aid than white people did. Some soup kitchens refused to serve black people.

Many black people worked in agriculture. Some owned land of their own. Many others rented land as sharecroppers. As the dust storms ripped up the Southern Plains, many sharecroppers could no longer pay their rent. They had few if any crops to sell. That meant they had to borrow more money to buy

5

Percentage of people who migrated to California during the Dust Bowl era who were black.

- The Great Depression affected black people severely.
- Harsh economic times meant black people faced even more discrimination.
- Most of the people who migrated west were white, while black people who did move away went north or east.

THINK ABOUT IT

Why do you think so few black people moved west to California during the Dust Bowl? Why did they choose to move to cities instead?

12

Some black people went east to work in Florida produce factories.

seeds and tools as they continued farming.

As things became more desperate, people from Oklahoma and Texas started moving west. But the vast majority of these people were white.

Black people who did move away from the Dust Bowl region were more likely to move north or east to cities such as Chicago, Illinois, and Detroit, Michigan.

5
Children Try to Stay Healthy

Life for children in the Dust Bowl region was not easy. They experienced many of the same problems faced by other people during the Great Depression. Their families often had very little money. There never seemed to be enough food to eat.

People who lived in the Dust Bowl breathed in lots of dust. The dust made many people sick. Children were especially at risk. As their lungs filled with dust, children developed asthma and

> People caught outside during dust storms would spit up dirt afterward.

7,000
Estimated number of people who died from dust pneumonia during the Dust Bowl era.

- The constant dust made many sick, but children were especially at risk for illness.
- Getting to and from school was challenging.
- Migrant children often had to work in the farm fields with their families.

14

pneumonia. Some children had to watch their siblings die from these diseases.

Getting to school was a challenge. Most children wore masks. Some walked to school backward to keep the dust from peppering their faces. Sometimes the schools kept the students overnight so they did not have to walk home during a dust storm, when they might get lost.

Life was not any easier for migrant children. Hunger and poverty were common outside the Dust Bowl. Children often had to work in the farm fields along with the rest of their family. They could spend several hours every day in the fields. There was no time for school.

This girl living in New Mexico herded cows for 5 cents a day to help support her family.

DANGEROUS ELECTRICITY

The dust storms were not dangerous just because of the dust. The dust built up static electricity as well. People could see blue flames shooting out of barbed wire fences. A shock could knock a person to the ground.

6

The Dust Bowl Affects More Than Farmers

The Dust Bowl region had been popular with settlers who wanted to farm. But they were not the only people living there. More than half of the people who lived there worked as teachers, lawyers, and small-business owners.

The failing farms had a big effect on these other businesses. A farmer who could not grow crops did not have money to pay for other things. Hardware store owners could not count on people to pay their bills. Grocery store owners had fewer customers.

Store owners had to sweep and shovel away dirt after every dust storm.

Many families packed up all of their belongings and left in search of work.

Farmers were also unable to pay their local taxes. Some county governments had to lay off police officers and teachers. Some local government offices closed altogether.

As businesses and professional offices closed, many of those people moved away. They looked for new jobs elsewhere. Many of them moved to California. They looked for work in cities. Some took money from federal aid programs. Many others found jobs in factories in their new home state.

266,229
Number of additional people who lived in Los Angeles, California, from 1930 to 1940.

- More than half the residents of the Dust Bowl region were not farmers.
- Some doctors and store owners also lost their businesses as people could not afford to buy things.
- Many of these people packed up and moved west, often settling in California.

7

California Residents Do Not Welcome Outsiders

In California, there were no dust storms. But the Great Depression still affected people living in the West. Money was scarce. Many people had lost their jobs. The harsh times meant some Californians took jobs they otherwise would not have. Sometimes the only jobs available were working as farmhands.

By the 1930s, many people from Mexico had arrived in California to work in the fields. When the Great Depression struck, some found that their jobs had been taken by white people. Many Mexican Americans were not US citizens. They could not receive government aid. Thousands of Mexican Americans had no choice but to move back to Mexico during the 1930s.

This Mexican American mother found work in California.

Migrants from the Dust Bowl and other areas showed up in California looking for work, too. Many Californians resented these new people looking for jobs. More than half of the people escaping the dust storms were not farmers.

Many had been successful in other areas of business. But the Californians lumped all migrants together. They called migrants Okies, insulted them, and mocked their southern accents. Some businesses separated Okies from the rest of their customers.

The Okies set up camps called Okievilles. Sometimes angry Californians came to the Okievilles. They beat up the migrants and burned down their shacks. The Californians feared that the migrants would take jobs away from them. Many of the migrants also had to accept government help to survive. This made many Californians resent the Okies even more.

25
Approximate percentage of Californians who were unemployed in 1933.

- California was affected by the Great Depression, making jobs and money scarce.
- Many Mexican Americans were forced to move back to Mexico after they lost their jobs.
- Californians feared Dust Bowl migrants would take away their jobs.
- Sometimes angry Californians burned down the shacks where the Dust Bowl migrants lived.

Many migrants lived in shacks that did not have electricity or plumbing.

8

California Government Tries to Stop Migrants

As migrants moved to new parts of the country, many state governments decided to take action. The government of California was no exception. California officials were worried that a large number of migrants would strain the state's resources.

In 1936, the Los Angeles police chief set up a border patrol. The patrol was called the Bum Brigade. Police officers in the patrol tried to stop the Dust Bowl migrants from entering California. They looked for people who did not appear to have any money or a job lined up.

Eventually the police chief was forced to remove the border patrol. The American Civil Liberties Union

Riots broke out in front of the Los Angeles County welfare office in 1934.

125

Number of police officers who were ordered to patrol in the Bum Brigade.

- Government officials in California worried migrants would make the state's financial problems even worse.
- The Los Angeles police department patrolled California's borders in 1936 to keep migrants out.
- County attorneys used the Indigent Act to charge local residents with a crime if they brought in poor relatives from other states.
- The ACLU challenged California's migrant laws.

This family was allowed into California only after borrowing $50 to show they had money.

(ACLU) sued the police department to get them to stop.

However, Californians found another way to try to stop the migrants from coming in. Politicians had passed the Indigent Act in 1933. This law made it a crime to bring people who were in poverty into the state of California. The law was not enforced much at first. But in 1939, attorneys from several California counties charged dozens of people with breaking the Indigent Act. These people had brought their poor relatives into California from other states. Many of the relatives came from the Dust Bowl region. The California residents were convicted. But once again, the ACLU challenged the law. That court case made it all the way to the US Supreme Court in 1941. It is now illegal for any state to restrict migration based on a person's income.

The US Government Finally Takes Action

At the beginning of the Dust Bowl era, politicians in Washington, DC, did not seem to notice what was happening. They were busy trying to solve the problems created by the Great Depression. By June 1933, however, problems in the Dust Bowl were too big to ignore.

President Franklin Delano Roosevelt created the Soil Erosion Service in 1933. Its director was Hugh Hammond Bennett. Bennett argued that farming methods had to change in order for the dust storms to stop. His criticism and plans angered some farmers. Some people in the US Congress were reluctant to consider spending federal money on different farming methods. But a dust storm traveled all the way to the East Coast in May 1934. Seeing a dust storm firsthand persuaded people in Congress to agree with Bennett. They passed the Soil Conservation Act in 1935. Bennett became the director of the Soil Conservation Service (SCS).

But Bennett still had to convince farmers to change their ways.

65
Percentage soil erosion was reduced by 1938.

- President Roosevelt created the Soil Erosion Service in 1933, and Hugh Hammond Bennett was its director.
- Bennett wanted to use new methods in agriculture, but farmers and the US Congress were not convinced at first.
- Congress passed the Soil Conservation Act of 1935 after a dust storm hit the East Coast.
- Farmers used Bennett's methods, and soil erosion slowed considerably.

This farmer listened to the SCS and planted elm trees to create a windbreak.

Through the SCS, farmers were encouraged to use contour plowing and terraces. They were also told to rotate crops instead of growing the same thing year after year. Most importantly, Bennett wanted farmers to leave some of their land unplowed. The roots from native prairie grasses would hold the soil in place.

Farmers who used Bennett's methods were more successful than those who did not. This encouraged them to stick to Bennett's plan. By 1938, the rate of soil erosion had slowed considerably. Finally, in 1940, the drought ended.

THE CIVILIAN CONSERVATION CORPS

In 1933, President Roosevelt created the Civilian Conservation Corps (CCC). The program hired more than 3.5 million young men. The CCC worked together with Bennett's SCS to plant trees on farmland. Planting lines of trees acted as a windbreak and kept some of the dust from blowing away.

10

The Media Begins to Pay Attention

In the 1930s, most people relied on newspapers and magazines for news. When the Dust Bowl era started, most journalists were not writing about agriculture. They were busy covering other topics. The whole country was suffering from the Great Depression. Many other countries were experiencing an economic depression, too.

But people from the Dust Bowl region began moving west in the mid-1930s. Some journalists began to notice the large number of migrants. A writer named Paul Taylor was one of the first to report on the many people arriving in California. He saw how difficult it was for these people to find jobs, homes, and food. He referred to them as refugees. Other journalists read Taylor's story. They began calling the migrants Dust Bowl refugees, too.

THINK ABOUT IT

What current events are not getting a lot of media attention? What responsibility does the media have to cover these types of events?

Paul Taylor testified before the US Congress about the need for the federal government to help migrant workers.

24

As the demand for jobs in California increased, so did conflict. Writers published stories covering the poor working and living conditions of the refugees. Photographers took heartbreaking photos. Journalists covered the battles fought by the state of California and its police departments to keep refugees out. The rest of the country noticed. By the end of the 1930s, the work done by the journalists had a tremendous impact.

Dorothea Lange's "Migrant Mother" remains one of the most widely recognized photos in the United States.

DOROTHEA LANGE

The Farm Security Administration hired Dorothea Lange to take pictures of rural California. Through her photography, the rest of the nation could see what life was really like for those who were poor. Many of the photos in this book were taken by Dorothea Lange. She is best known for her photo called "Migrant Mother." It shows an out-of-work pea picker.

1935

Year the term *Dust Bowl* first appeared in a newspaper column.

- Journalists were slow to cover the problems of the Dust Bowl because of the Great Depression.
- Paul Taylor was one of the first reporters to write about what was happening in California.
- More journalists wanted to cover the Dust Bowl and the migrants who moved west.
- Newspaper articles helped influence public opinion about the migrants.

25

11 Artists Want to Tell Dust Bowl Stories

As the country learned more about the Dust Bowl, many artists felt drawn to the area and its migrants. Woody Guthrie was living in Texas when the Dust Bowl era began. He moved to California and worked in a bar. In his free time, Guthrie performed at farms where other migrants worked. He was shocked at the way workers were treated. His anger began to show up in the songs he wrote. His song "This Land Is Your Land" is still famous today. His music earned him the nickname Dust Bowl Troubadour.

Alexandre Hogue grew up in Texas. He watched as people left to find a

Woody Guthrie

ARTISTS AND THE WPA

The Works Progress Administration (WPA) was created in 1935. Most employees built bridges, roads, and buildings. But part of the WPA work consisted of creating art. Over the span of eight years, WPA artists created 2,566 murals and 17,744 pieces of sculpture.

The Grapes of Wrath was made into a movie in 1940.

better life in the West. His paintings of dust, erosion, and crooked fence posts capture the desolation caused by the drought and dust storms.

John Steinbeck wrote a novel called *The Grapes of Wrath*. It was about a fictional family who had been forced from their farm in Oklahoma. Thousands of people read the novel. It helped them understand the hardships faced by migrants, including people who left the Dust Bowl. The book immediately became a best seller. Steinbeck later went on to win the Pulitzer Prize for fiction.

430,000
Number of copies *The Grapes of Wrath* sold in 1939, the year it was first published.

- Many artists were drawn to the stories of Dust Bowl survivors and migrants.
- Woody Guthrie came from the Dust Bowl and eventually became a famous folk singer who sang about the migrants.
- Alexandre Hogue painted the desolation caused by the drought and dust storms.
- John Steinbeck wrote *The Grapes of Wrath* about a migrant family.

12 California Farms Benefit from Law Exclusions

Many farms in California were owned by large companies. Some of them did not like hiring people with Mexican or Asian heritage. Most Dust Bowl migrants were white, so the companies preferred to hire them instead. Due to the large number of people seeking jobs, companies could also offer their workers lower pay. There was always someone desperate enough to take the job.

Some Dust Bowl migrants would camp alongside the road, waiting for the next crop harvest to begin.

Workers pull crates of lettuce off trucks as part of a strike in 1936.

2.36
Number of available workers for each job in California in 1933.

- When the Dust Bowl migrants came to California, large farms could afford to stop hiring people from Mexico to work in the fields.
- Dust Bowl migrants stayed in California after harvest time ended.
- Some large farms feared the migrants would form unions and strike.
- Laws passed in the 1930s that protected other workers often did not apply to hired farmhands.

Until the mid-1930s, the large farms in California depended on workers from Mexico to pick cotton and other crops. After the harvest, some of these workers would return to Mexico. But the Dust Bowl migrants were often families, not just individuals. After harvest time ended, they stayed in California.

The large farm owners feared that the growing number of migrants might try to form a union. If they did, they might try to demand better wages. But the farm owners did not have to worry. The US Congress passed the National Labor Relations Act in 1935. This gave many workers the right to form unions. But farm workers were specifically excluded from this law. Additionally, Congress passed the first minimum wage law in 1938. Once again, the law did not apply to farmhands.

29

Glossary

agriculture
Farming.

brigade
A group of people who organize to take action together.

contour plowing
Plowing rows that follow the land's curve rather than going straight up or down, which forms ridges that help keep soil in place.

drought
A long period of time when no rain or other precipitation falls.

exclude
To keep out.

farmhand
A person who is hired to work on a farm.

migrant
A person who moves from one place to another to find work.

persuade
To convince.

poverty
Being very poor.

skeptical
Having doubts.

strike
An act by a group of employees who organize a work stoppage in order to demand changes in working conditions or wages.

terrace
A flat area created on the side of a hill and used to grow crops.

For More Information

Books

Brown, Don. *The Great American Dust Bowl.* New York: Houghton Mifflin Harcourt, 2013.

Garland, Sherry. *Voices of the Dust Bowl.* Gretna, LA: Pelican Publishing, 2012.

Marrin, Albert. *Years of Dust: The Story of the Dust Bowl.* New York: Dutton Children's Books, 2009.

Visit 12StoryLibrary.com

Scan the code or use your school's login at **12StoryLibrary.com** for recent updates about this topic and a full digital version of this book. Enjoy free access to:

- Digital ebook
- Breaking news updates
- Live content feeds
- Videos, interactive maps, and graphics
- Additional web resources

Note to educators: Visit 12StoryLibrary.com/register to sign up for free premium website access. Enjoy live content plus a full digital version of every 12-Story Library book you own for every student at your school.

Index

American Civil Liberties
Union (ACLU), 21

Bennett, Hugh
Hammond, 22–23
Black Sunday, 9
border patrol, 20

California, 10, 11, 17,
18–19, 20–21, 24,
25, 26, 28–29
children, 9, 14–15
Civilian Conservation
Corps (CCC), 23

drought, 6–7, 10, 23, 27
dust storms, 6, 8, 9, 10,
12, 15, 18, 22, 27

Grapes of Wrath, The, 27
Great Depression, 8, 10,
12, 14, 18, 22, 24
Guthrie, Woody, 26

Hogue, Alexandre,
26–27

Indigent Act (1933), 21

journalists, 24–25

Lange, Dorothea, 25

Mexico, 18, 29
migrant workers, 10–11,
15, 18, 19, 20–21,
24, 25, 26, 27, 28,
29

National Labor Relations
Act (1935), 29

Okies, 10–11, 19
Oklahoma, 10, 13, 27

Roosevelt, Franklin
Delano, 22, 23

Soil Conservation
Service (SCS), 22, 23
Soil Erosion Service
(SES), 22
Steinbeck, John, 27

terraces, 6, 23
Texas, 13, 26
"This Land Is Your Land,"
26

US government, 6, 10,
22–23
US Supreme Court, 21

Works Progress
Administration (WPA),
26

About the Author

Amy C. Rea grew up in northern
Minnesota and now lives in a
Minneapolis suburb with her husband,
two sons, and dog. She writes
frequently about traveling around
Minnesota. She has also written books
about US history.

READ MORE FROM 12-STORY LIBRARY

Every 12-Story Library book
is available in many formats.
For more information, visit
12StoryLibrary.com.